Cookin'
in the
Kitchen

D0815890

Cookin'
in the
Kitchen

Jenny Bristow

Appletree Press

For my family

First published by
The Appletree Press Ltd
19-21 Alfred Street
Belfast BT2 8DL
1995

Photographer: Kenneth McNally
Food stylist: Anne Bryan
Illustrations: Des Fox
Typesetting: Paragon Typesetters
Printed in Ireland by ColourBooks Ltd.

A catalogue record for this book
is available from the British Library.

ISBN 0 86281 581 9

9 8 7 6 5 4 3 2 1

Contents

Preface 7

Acknowledgements 8

1 The Soup Kitchen 9

2 Simply Saucy 25

3 Cracking Good Ideas with Eggs 41

4 A Good Roasting 57

5 Going with the Grain 75

6 Perfecting the Pasta 93

7 Game for Christmas 107

Preface

This book is for everyone, regardless of their culinary ability. It follows my ethos of life, which is that it's best if kept simple. Why complicate dishes unnecessarily, when excellent results can be achieved by preparing good, fresh ingredients in simple and relaxed ways?

Cooking for me is a passion, yet I appreciate only too well that for many it can be a tedious chore. Nevertheless cooking trends have evolved greatly in recent years and for many it is now possible to combine the demands of feeding a family with the need for good, healthy food.

Today, more than ever, we realise that food is also one of our best medicines and needs to be treated and cooked with care. My recipes combine common sense with good, healthy eating, bearing in mind that a good diet is often a question of balance, rather than the avoidance of certain foods. As in so many other areas of life, a little of most foods in moderation is frequently the best policy. There are recipes in this book for the vegetarian, the budget-conscious and coeliacs, in addition to those of you looking for good, robustly-flavoured food that brings comfort and pleasure to both body and soul.

Flavours vary more than ever now that the range of foods on our supermarket shelves is so great, and this helps inspire our cooking. I have included many new ideas for filling soups; modern and easy-to-prepare pasta dishes; the simple roasting of fish and vegetable dishes, as well as meats; cereals and grain, used in a variety of ways; varied uses for eggs, both for snacks and main meals; uncomplicated sauces; and many new recipes for the Christmas season, with the focus on game and painless ways to celebrate Christmas in festive style.

The recipes contained here have given me yet another opportunity to share my genuine love of cooking with a wider audience, and I hope you will derive at least some of the pleasure from them that they have given me.

Acknowledgements

Filming another cookery series and writing the book simultaneously has not been an easy task, so I have learned to rely and depend upon the art of gentle persuasion, accepting the help and encouragement of many people to meet rapidly approaching deadlines.

Firstly, I thank my producer, Ruth Johnston, whose unending supply of inspiration and encouragement made it all happen.

As ever, I am grateful to UTV for the opportunity to make another cookery series and my thanks to the UTV crew, Sam Christie, Rai Woods, Brian Armstrong, Patricia Moore, Felicity Clements, Valerie Lamrock and Philip White. They became a way of life in Cullybackey.

My thanks to photographer, Ken McNally, and the food stylist, Anne Bryan.

Also to the invaluable helpers behind the scene: Maureen Best, Sally Stirling, Donna Boyd, Joanne Hughes.

To Vera McCready who typed the text; to my editor, Douglas Marshall, who managed to apply the right amount of pressure to deliver the final manuscript on time, and to Nicola Lavery, who copy-edited the text.

Part of the charm of the television series has been the variety of dishes, pots, pans, jugs, utensils and, of course, flowers. My thanks to Sally Backus of Floral Design, Lorna Bassett of Honeysuckle, Mary Kelso of Warden's, David Flynn of Marlborough Antiques, Christine Foy from Mulaghmeen Pottery, Pat McNeill of Beeswax Interiors, Bailie and Irwin of Paint Effects, Maisie Duncan at Le Creuset, Michelle Kershaw from Lakeland Plastics, Albert Forsythe, June Revill and my long-established cooking friends from Calor Gas, Maud Hamill and Ian McKay.

Thank you all for your help.

Jenny

1

The Soup Kitchen

W hether you think of soup as a starter, a comforting filler or as a meal in itself, for me soup—served in the kitchen—lies at the very heart of family cooking. There are recipes here for a whole range of soups which you can serve hot or cold, either at the beginning or at the end of a meal.

Recipes

· *Bean and Ham Broth with Golden Soda Bread*

· *Portavogie Bouillabaisse*

· *Cream of Onion Soup*

· *Saturday Soup*

· *Rustic Gingered Carrot Soup*

· *Pumpkin, Orange and Hazelnut Soup*

· *Mushroom Soup under a Cheese Crust*

· *Caramelised Apricot Soup with Toasted Almonds*

Bean and Ham Broth with Golden Soda Bread

This is a really filling soup at any time of the day. Try serving it with crispy golden soda bread as an extra garnish.

[Serves 6-8]

HAM STOCK
750g (1½lb) ham shank
2½l (4pt) water
1 onion, cut into quarters
small bunch of parsley

SOUP
500g (1lb) dried butter or haricot beans
1l (2pt) water
2 onions, finely chopped
4 stalks of celery, chopped
1 dsp oil
250g (8oz) ham flesh, roughly chopped
salt and pepper
pinch paprika
2½l (4pt) ham stock, strained
2 spring onions, finely chopped (optional)
2 dsp parsley, finely chopped
150ml (5fl oz) cream (optional)
1 soda farl
3 dsp olive oil

OVERNIGHT PREPARATION
Soak the ham shank overnight in cold water to remove excess salt. In a separate dish, cover the dried beans with 1l (2pt) cold water and soak overnight.

TO MAKE THE STOCK
After soaking, place the ham in a large saucepan, cover with cold water and bring to the boil. Change the water and bring to the boil again. This process will ensure that any excess salt is removed from the ham shank. Then place the ham in a large saucepan and cover with 2½l (4pt) cold water. Add the onion and the parsley and bring to the boil. Cover and simmer for 30-35 minutes. Stir

occasionally and skim any scum from the surface of the water. Strain and reserve stock. Remove the ham flesh from the bone, chop and set aside.

TO MAKE THE SOUP

In a saucepan, sweat the onion and celery in the oil for 8-10 minutes, until softened and opaque, but not coloured. Add the seasoning, paprika and half of the soaked beans. Cook for a few minutes before adding the stock. Blend the soup and then return to the saucepan. Add the remaining beans, stock, chopped ham, spring onions, parsley and, if desired, a little cream.

Cut the soda farl into quarters, and fry in hot olive oil until crispy and golden. Drain on kitchen paper, and serve hot with the soup.

Portavogie Bouillabaisse

This French-Mediterranean soup has endless variations depending on the region in which it is made. My version includes the usual basic ingredients; good fresh fish, garlic, olive oil and saffron, but no tomatoes.

[*Serves 6-8*]

FISH STOCK
5l (8pt) cold water
1kg (2lb) assorted fish trimmings (bones, heads, skin)
3 spring onion bulbs
outer peelings of a fennel bulb
1 small leek, cut into quarters
150ml (5fl oz) dry white wine
3 strips lemon peel
4 peppercorns

SOUP
2 tbsp olive oil
3 cloves garlic, crushed
250g (8oz) fennel, cut into strips
4 dsp spring onion bulbs, chopped

250g (8oz) potatoes, cubed
5l (8pt) fish stock
150ml (5fl oz) dry white wine
10 strands saffron, soaked in 4 dsp boiling water
1kg (2lb) assorted firm-fleshed fish and shellfish
(e.g. monkfish, cod, haddock, mussels, peeled prawns or shrimps)
salt and pepper

To Serve
60ml (2fl oz) cream
2 tbsp parsley or dill, chopped

To Make The Stock

Put the water, fish trimmings, vegetables, wine, lemon peel and peppercorns into a large saucepan. Bring slowly to the boil, skimming often, and then simmer gently for 35-45 minutes, being careful not to overcook, as excess boiling will break up the fish bones and the stock will take on an unpleasant flavour. Strain through muslin to remove any solids. This stock freezes extremely well.

To Make The Soup

In a separate pan, heat the olive oil and garlic then add the fennel strips and spring onions. Cook for 4-5 minutes and then add the cubed potatoes, stock, wine, saffron and shellfish and cook for 8-10 minutes. If using mussels, discard any which have not opened. Cut the fish into cubes and place in a steamer. Cook gently for 1-2 minutes, being careful not to let the fish to break up. Add the fish cubes to the bouillabaisse, season and heat through.

Serve hot with a swirl of cream and a sprinkling of the chopped herbs.

Overleaf: Portavogie Bouillabaisse (left) and Cream of Onion Soup (right)

Cream of Onion Soup

Onions make a good basis for an economical, yet tasty, soup with a lovely texture. I prefer the flavour of Spanish onions in this dish.

[*Serves 8*]

4 large onions, finely chopped
1 bay leaf, crushed
30g (1oz) butter
2 dsp oil
1 tsp sugar
50g (1½oz) plain flour
300ml (10fl oz) white wine
1½l (3pts) chicken stock
salt and pepper
300ml (10fl oz) cream

TO SERVE
sprigs of parsley
peppercorns, ground

Sweat the onion and crushed bay leaf in the butter and the oil for 8-10 minutes until softened. Add the sugar and flour, and mix well. Then add the white wine and stock and stir well. Cover and simmer gently for 30 minutes. Liquidise or blend the mixture and add seasoning.

Serve hot with a swirl of cream and a sprig of parsley dusted with crushed peppercorns.

Saturday Soup

A hearty lunchtime soup for hungry mouths after the exertions of a Saturday morning. The basis of this soup is a can of potato-based soup.

[Serves 6-8]

SOUP
300ml (10fl oz) water or milk
2 tins potato-based soup, puréed
125g (4oz) Savoy cabbage, shredded
250g (8oz) parsnips, sliced
1 egg, beaten
1 dsp oil
1 carrot, diced
250g (8oz) chicken, cooked and diced
375g (12oz) mixed pulses
(split green and yellow peas, split green lentils)
soaked in water for 1 hour

TO SERVE
boiled potatoes (optional)
2 dsp parsley, finely chopped

Stir the water or milk into the soup puree to thin. Blanch the cabbage and parsnips in boiling water for 1 minute. Then brush the parsnip with egg, sprinkle with oil, and roast in the oven, gas mark 5, 375°F, 190°C, for 8-10 minutes or until golden. Boil the diced carrot for 4-5 minutes. Add the cabbage, carrots, parsnips, diced chicken and the drained pulses to the soup puree. Heat for 15 minutes.

This soup is particularly good served over a hot floury potato, garnished with parsley.

Rustic Gingered Carrot Soup

In this economical soup the flavour of carrot combines well with the dry-roasted spices and hint of ginger. It is at its very best when carrots are in season and are small and sweet, but it tastes good at any time of the year.

[*Serves 6*]

1½l (3pt) water
2 vegetable stock cubes
1 dsp olive oil
1 clove garlic, chopped
2cm- (1 inch-) cube of root ginger, peeled and finely chopped
1 tsp coriander seed
1 tsp mustard seeds
1oz butter or margarine
1kg (2lb) carrots, finely grated

Boil the water, add the stock cubes and set aside. Heat the oil in a large saucepan and gently cook the garlic and the ginger for several minutes until softened. In a separate small pan, dry-roast the coriander and mustard seeds. You will know they are ready when they pop in the pan. Gently crush the seeds and reserve 1 teaspoonful. Add the remainder to the garlic and ginger. Add the butter to the saucepan and then the grated carrots. Cook until the carrots are glazed and soft. Add the stock and simmer for a further 10-12 minutes, then blend the mixture until smooth.

Serve at once, garnished with a sprinkling of the reserved dry-roasted seeds.

Pumpkin, Orange and Hazelnut Soup

An unusual and robust soup with quite a unique texture. I use blood oranges when they are available as their intense flavour adds a sharpness to the soup. The hazelnuts must be really fresh, so if you can, buy them in their shells and grind them to a fine powder using a coffee grinder or a pestle and mortar. I have been known to use a rolling pin!

As an extra novelty, this soup can be returned to the pumpkin shell and kept warm in the oven. If you intend doing this, be careful when scooping out the flesh not to puncture the side of the pumpkin. This soup freezes very well.

[Serves 6-8]

1½kg (3lbs) pumpkin flesh
2 dsp walnut or olive oil
15g (½oz) butter or margarine
1 clove garlic, crushed
1 onion, chopped
4 spring onion bulbs, finely chopped
1l (2pt) chicken or vegetable stock
salt and pepper
juice of 2 oranges
rind of 1 orange
125g (4oz) hazelnuts, finely ground

TO SERVE
1 spring onion bulb, finely chopped
1dsp hazelnuts, finely chopped

Prepare the pumpkin by cutting off the top, removing the seeds and scooping out the flesh from the inside. Dice 3lb of the pumpkin flesh and set aside. (Any remaining flesh can be frozen.) Heat the oil and butter in a saucepan and add the crushed garlic, onion, spring onions and diced pumpkin and sweat for 2-3 minutes. Cook over a low heat, stirring well for a further 5 minutes. Add the stock and simmer for 1 hour until the flesh of the pumpkin is soft. Blend or sieve the soup and return to the saucepan. Add the salt and pepper, orange juice and rind, and the hazelnuts. Reheat gently for 5-10 minutes before serving.

Serve sprinkled with a little finely chopped hazelnut and spring onion.

Mushroom Soup under a Cheese Crust

This hearty soup has a rather chunky texture but, if you prefer, you can process it in a blender to make it smoother. The unusual cheese crust topping is optional, but it is delicious.

[Serves 6-8]

Chicken Stock
1 boiling chicken (approximately 3lb)
3l (5pt) water
½ onion, roughly chopped
1 carrot, roughly chopped
1 stalk of celery, broken in half
salt and pepper

Soup
1kg (2lb) button mushrooms, finely sliced
1 large onion, finely chopped
1 dsp olive oil
30g (1oz) butter
50g (1½oz) plain flour mixed with 4 dsp warm water
300ml (10fl oz) milk
2l (3pt) chicken stock

Cheese Crust
250g (8oz) plain flour
50g (1½oz) butter or margarine
60g (2oz) grated goat's or sheep's cheese (eg Bennings or Etorki)
2 eggs, beaten
1 egg yolk
cold water to bind

To Make The Stock
This is a very useful stock and can be made in larger quantities and stored in the freezer until needed. Place the chicken in a large stock pot and add the water and other stock ingredients. Bring to the boil and then simmer gently for approximately 2 hours to give a really concentrated stock. Strain the stock and keep it cool.

TO MAKE THE SOUP

In a saucepan, sweat the mushrooms and the onion in the oil and butter until softened. Add the flour and water mixture; this will prevent lumps forming when the stock is added. Next add the milk and the stock; stir until the soup thickens and is bubbling. Season and leave to simmer for 15 minutes.

TO MAKE THE CRUST

Sieve the flour into a bowl, cut and rub in the butter or margarine. Add the cheese, half of the beaten egg, the egg yolk, and enough water to bind to stiff, firm dough. Roll out dough to a thickness of 1cm (½ inch), then cut the pastry lid to fit the serving dish (allow a 3 cm (1 inch) border for sealing). Leave the dough to relax for 30 minutes.

Preheat oven to gas mark 6, 400°F, 200°C. Pour the soup into an oven-proof serving dish. Brush the edges of the pastry lid with a little beaten egg and place on the dish, sealing the edges well. Make a split in the centre of the pastry lid and glaze with beaten egg. Bake for 25 minutes or until golden.   Serve hot with small chunks of the crust.

Mushroom Soup under a Cheese Crust

Caramelised Apricot Soup with Toasted Almonds

Here soup is served as a light delicious pudding. This recipe works equally well with other fruits.

[Serves 3-4]

1 large tin of apricots in their juice
100ml (3fl oz) sweet dessert wine or fruit juice
pinch cinnamon
30g (1oz) butter or margarine
50g (1½oz) soft brown sugar
4 fresh apricots, sliced

TO SERVE
1 dsp yoghurt
30g (1oz) toasted flaked almonds

In a saucepan, heat the tinned apricots, their juice and the wine or fruit juice until the fruit is soft and tender. Transfer to a blender and puree until mixture is thin, then add the cinamon and a little extra wine or fruit juice until the mixture is of a pouring consistency. In a separate saucepan, heat the butter and brown sugar together until they caramelise and are gold and bubbling. Add the sliced fresh apricots to the caramel and toss until golden brown. Arrange the caramelised apricots at the bottom of the serving dish, then ladle the apricot soup carefully over the top.

Decorate with a swirl of yoghurt and a sprinkle of toasted almonds.

2
Simply Saucy

T he thought of making a sauce scares the wits out of a lot of people. But it need not, as the trend in cookery is towards making sauces simple, light and uncomplicated, whether they are to dress meat, fish, salads or puddings.

Recipes

· *Leek-filled Plaice with a Rich Butter Sauce*
· *Crispy Noodles and Stir-fried Vegetables with Honey and Chilli Sauce*
· *Salad of Iceberg Lettuce with Sweet Poppy Seed Dressing*
· *Seafood Platter with a Tangy Sauce*
· *Grilled Fillet Steak with Chasseur Sauce*
· *Yoghurt-coated Chicken Wings with a Mustard and Cream Sauce*
· *An Old-fashioned Vanilla Custard Cake*
· *Rich Dark Chocolate Sauce*
· *Hot Biscuit Sauce*

Leek-filled Plaice with a Rich Butter Sauce

Fish need a sauce with a certain sharpness of flavour, and this sauce is a particularly good compliment to the flavours of this plaice dish. It is important that the butter is firm and very cold.

[Serves 5]

LEEK-FILLED PLAICE
15g (½oz) butter
1 leek, cut finely into rings
5 plaice fillets
black pepper
150ml (5fl oz) dry white wine

BUTTER SAUCE
200g (6oz) butter
3 spring onion bulbs, chopped
300ml (10fl oz) dry white wine
4 dsp cream
salt and pepper
1 dsp spring onions, finely chopped
1 dsp leek, cooked and finely sliced

Preheat oven to gas mark 6, 400°F, 200°C. Melt the butter in a small saucepan and fry the leek rings for 1 minute to improve their colour. Spread the leek and butter mixture over the fish fillets and roll each one up from the tail to the head. Place in a lightly-greased ovenproof dish, sprinkle with pepper and pour over the white wine to poach the fish fillets. Cook in the oven for 30 minutes.

TO MAKE THE SAUCE
Melt a knob of butter in the saucepan and gently fry the spring onion bulbs for 1 minute. Add the white wine and boil to reduce the liquid by half: this helps to concentrate the flavour. Add the cream and bring to the boil. Cool slightly before adding the rest of the butter in small pieces, whisking well between each addition. When all the butter has been incorporated, sprinkle the chopped spring onion, seasoning and leek into the sauce for extra colour.

Serve hot with the sauce poured over the fish rolls.

Crispy Noodles and Vegetables with Honey and Chilli Sauce

A well-flavoured sauce is often all that is needed to turn a simple platter of fresh vegetables into a tasty main course. I am especially fond of the tangy combination of honey and chilli.

[Serves 6]

HONEY AND CHILLI SAUCE
2 dsp sesame oil
750g (1½lb) assorted vegetables
(cauliflower and broccoli florets, sliced mushrooms,
diced peppers, onion rings and chopped celery)
2cm- (1 inch-) cube of root ginger, finely chopped
1 dsp chilli sauce
2 dsp honey
1 dsp soy sauce
1 tsp cornflour blended with 2 dsp water
150ml (5fl oz) vegetable stock
2 dsp spring onions, finely chopped

CRISPY NOODLES
1l (2 pts) water
pinch of salt
250g (8oz) egg noodles
2 dsp olive oil

Heat the sesame oil in a large frying pan or a wok and then add the vegetables. Toss them in the hot oil until they are well-coated and lightly cooked. Add the chopped ginger, chilli sauce, honey, soy sauce, cornflour and vegetable stock to the vegetables and bring to the boil, before simmering for 3 minutes.

Put the water and salt into a large saucepan and bring to the boil. Add the egg noodles and boil for 5 minutes before draining and patting them dry. Heat the oil in a large frying pan or wok, add the noodles and toss until crispy and golden.

Serve the vegetables hot sprinkled with spring onions and accompanied by crispy noodles.

Salad of Iceberg Lettuce with Sweet Poppy Seed Dressing

This dressing can be made with standard Spanish onions but I prefer to use red onions. By varying the vinegar you use, you can have different coloured dressings.

[Serves 6]

1 iceberg lettuce, washed and separated
4 dsp olive or grapeseed oil
4 dsp red wine vinegar
1 small red onion, finely chopped
2 dsp caster sugar
½ tsp dried mustard
salt and pepper
1 dsp poppy seeds

Put all the ingredients, except the poppy seeds, into a food processor. Pulse until well blended, then add the poppy seeds and mix by hand. Pour over the lettuce.

Overleaf: Iceberg Lettuce Salad (left) and Seafood Platter (right)

Seafood Platter with a Tangy Sauce

This dish can be made using a variety of fish, from the simple to the more exotic. I have used turbot and salmon. The delicious seafood sauce combines equally well with both, and can be made using low-calorie mayonnaise and yoghurt. Fish is best served at room temperature, never straight from the fridge.

[*Serves 6*]

750g (1½lb) turbot and salmon fillets
2 dsp lemon juice
black pepper

TANGY SAUCE
250g (8oz) mayonnaise
120g (4oz) yoghurt or cream
1 tsp paprika
1 dsp tomato puree
2 dsp lemon juice
few drops Tabasco sauce
250g (8oz) prawns, cooked and peeled
120g (4oz) cucumber, diced
1 dsp spring onions, finely chopped
1 dsp peppercorns, lightly crushed
1 dsp cornflour blended with 2 dsp water (optional)

Cut the fish into bite-sized pieces then place in a steamer. Sprinkle with lemon juice and black pepper and leave to steam for 4 minutes over gently boiling water. When cooked arrange on a platter.

In a large bowl, mix the mayonnaise, yoghurt or cream, paprika, tomato puree, lemon juice and Tabasco sauce. (This basic sauce can keep in the fridge for up to one week if stored in an airtight jar.) Add the prawns, cucumbers, spring onions, peppercorns and mix well. Pour the sauce over the fish and serve cold.

If you would like to serve this dish warm, add 1 tsp cornflour mixed with 2 dsp water to the mayonnaise, so that during heating the cornflour will stabilise the yoghurt or cream. Heat in the oven at gas mark 4, 350°F, 180°C for 10 minutes

Grilled Fillet Steak
with Chasseur Sauce

This sauce has the most wonderful aroma and is easy to cook. The meat is cooked separately on a grill where the rich meat juices form the basis of this sauce.

[Serves 2]

1 dsp oil or butter
salt and pepper
2 fillet steaks, 3cm (1½ inch) thick

CHASSEUR SAUCE
4 dsp meat juices
1 clove garlic, very finely chopped
2 dsp spring onions, very finely chopped
60g (2oz) mushrooms, sliced
150ml (5fl oz) white wine
1 dsp brandy
1 dsp tomato puree
1 tsp arrowroot blended with 2 dsp water
2 tomatoes, skinned, de-seeded and chopped
sprig of fresh tarragon

Heat the oil or butter under a grill, season the steaks and then grill them on both sides, at the highest setting, to seal in the juices. Reduce the temperature and cook according to individual preference: rare, medium or well-done.

While the steaks are cooking, prepare the sauce: drain the meat juices from the pan, put 4 dsp into a saucepan and add the garlic, spring onions and mushrooms. Cook for 1 minute before adding the white wine, brandy, tomato puree, arrowroot, tomatoes and tarragon. Reduce the heat and allow to simmer gently for 8 minutes.

Serve sauce hot poured over the steaks.

Overleaf: Grilled Fillet Steak (left) and Yoghurt-coated Chicken Wings (right)

Yoghurt-coated Chicken Wings with a Mustard and Cream Sauce

Chicken wings are becoming very popular as a tasty starter, and this marinade and sauce compliment each other perfectly. I find that the flesh on the wings cooks best by roasting in the oven.

[Serves 6]

12 chicken wings
250g (8oz) Greek yoghurt
3 cloves of garlic, crushed
pinch paprika
rind and juice of half an orange
pinch salt and pepper
olive oil

MUSTARD AND CREAM SAUCE
4 dsp chicken juices
rind and juice of half an orange
pinch paprika
300ml (10fl oz) cream
2 tsp wholegrain mustard

Preheat the oven to gas mark 5, 375°F, 190°C. Trim the wing tips from the chicken joints, and make slits along the wings at intervals. Blend together the yoghurt, garlic, paprika, orange juice and rind, salt and pepper. Add the wings to the marinade and toss well, then transfer to a large roasting dish. Flatten out each wing to ensure even cooking and drizzle a little olive oil over each. Cook in the oven for 1 hour or until the chicken is tender.

Remove 4 dsp of chicken juices from the roasting dish and heat gently in a small saucepan. Add the orange juice and rind, paprika, cream and mustard and mix well. Do not overheat or the sauce will become thin.

Serve the sauce hot either poured over the chicken wings or in a separate sauceboat.

An Old-fashioned Vanilla Custard Cake

An elegant pudding whose origin lies in a bowl of custard flavoured with praline, sherry, and almond-flavoured biscuits. You can substitute the almond biscuits for sponge fingers if you would like to change the texture of this pudding.

[Serves 8]

PRALINE
60g (2oz) whole almonds
2 dsp water
60g (2oz) sugar

VANILLA EGG CUSTARD
450ml (15fl oz) milk
6 egg yolks
6 dsp caster sugar
few drops of vanilla essence
2 dsp sherry
1 dsp arrowroot mixed with 1 dsp water
30g (1oz) gelatine
2 dsp water
300ml (10fl oz) whipped cream
125g (4oz) ratafia biscuits
sherry

Place the almonds, water and sugar in a small saucepan and boil rapidly for 8 minutes, until the mixture turns golden and resembles toffee. Pour on to a sheet of greaseproof paper and allow to harden before chopping finely.

Warm the milk in a saucepan. Beat the egg yolks and caster sugar together until light and creamy, then whisk into the milk. Beat well over a low heat before adding the vanilla essence, sherry and arrowroot. Heat until the custard thickens, then strain through a sieve and leave to cool. Put the gelatine and water into a small bowl and place this in a pan of warm, but not boiling, water. Stir until the gelatine is completely dissolved and then add to the custard with the chopped praline and the cream. Mix well before pouring half the mixture into a loose-bottomed 18cm (7 inch) cake tin. Place the ratafia biscuits on a plate and drizzle with the sherry. Arrange the biscuits on top of the custard layer and then pour the remaining custard on top. Chill in the fridge for 2 hours or until firm, then unmould. Serve decorated with chopped praline and whipped cream

Rich Dark Chocolate Sauce

A sauce full of flavour that holds its consistency as it cools down. Chocolate sauce combines well with ice cream, fresh fruit or a simple steamed chocolate pudding.

[Serves 4]

125g (4oz) dark chocolate
100ml (3fl oz) water
30g (1oz) caster sugar
1 tsp arrowroot, mixed with 2 tsp cold water
1 tsp vanilla essence
15g (½oz) butter
3 tbsp cream

Melt the chocolate by heating in a bowl placed over a saucepan of boiling water. Add the water and mix well before adding the sugar, arrowroot, vanilla, butter and cream. Beat until the sauce takes on a smooth, shiny texture.

This sauce is best served hot.

Hot Biscuit Sauce

This sauce turns vanilla ice cream into a special treat at any time of the year but it is particularly good during the festive season when quick, light puddings are so often called for. The crumbled biscuits in this sauce give it a most attractive texture.

[*Serves 8*]

4 egg yolks
60g (2oz) caster sugar
½ tsp vanilla essence
100ml (3fl oz) sweet white wine
4 dsp almond essence or Amaretto liqueur
150ml (5fl oz) double cream, lightly whipped
4 small Amaretto or almond-flavoured biscuits, crumbled

Beat together the egg yolks and caster sugar in a heat- resistant bowl until light and fluffy. Place the bowl over a saucepan of boiling water and continue to beat the egg mixture, adding the vanilla and wine. The sauce will increase in volume after about 8 minutes. Remove from the heat and add the almond essence or liqueur and the cream.

Just before serving stir in the biscuit crumbs, and pour over ice cream.

3
Cracking Good Ideas with Eggs

Boiled, poached, scrambled, fried, mousses, omelettes, sauces, not to mention all sorts of cakes and biscuits. What would we do without eggs!

Recipes

· *Mediterranean Fruit 'n' Nut Chicken*

· *Vanilla and Cinnamon French Toast*

· *An Old-time Egg and Fish Pie*

· *Peppered Bacon and Eggs*

· *Tasty Family Omelette*

· *Soufflé Omelette*

· *A Freezing Hot Pudding*

· *One-mix Victoria Sponge Cake*

· *Old-fashioned Lemon Curd*

· *Irish Whiskey Syllabub*

Mediterranean Fruit 'n' Nut Chicken

This light chicken dish is ideal for a party or special occasion. You can use whatever fruits are in season, or even a combination of fresh and tinned fruit. The marinade ensures that the chicken is moist and flavoursome when cooked.

[Serves 6-8]

LIME-FLAVOURED MAYONNAISE
1 whole egg
4 egg yolks
1 tsp dry mustard
½ tsp salt
300ml (10fl oz) light olive oil
2 tsp white wine vinegar
3 dsp lime or lemon juice
300ml (10fl oz) yoghurt, cream or fromage frais
½ tsp paprika
pinch black pepper

MARINATED CHICKEN
750g (1½lb) chicken pieces
2 dsp honey
2 cloves garlic, chopped
2 dsp olive oil
60g (2oz) hazelnuts, halved

FRUIT AND VEGETABLE BASE
750g (1½lb) assorted fresh fruit, peeled and sliced
2 spring onions, finely chopped
2 stalks celery, finely sliced

Prepare the mayonnaise by beating the whole egg and the egg yolks over a pan of hot water for 10-12 minutes until the eggs are cooked, being careful not to let them curdle. Transfer to a blender, add the mustard and salt and slowly pour in the oil a little at a time until the mayonnaise thickens. Add the vinegar and blend again. Thin the mayonnaise by adding the lime or lemon juice and the yoghurt or cream. Season with paprika and black pepper.

Cut the chicken into bite-sized pieces and place in a bowl with the honey, garlic, hazelnut and olive oil. Stir and leave to marinate for 3-4 hours. Transfer the chicken and marinade to a saucepan and fry for 10 minutes or until the chicken is golden brown. Add the hazelnuts and fry for another 2 minutes. Allow to cool.

Arrange the fruit and vegetables on a serving platter, pour over the chicken and marinade mixture. Cover with the lime-flavoured mayonnaise and garnish with a little spring onion and toasted hazelnuts.

Serve chilled or slightly warm.

Vanilla and Cinnamon French Toast

This is a quick snack, easy to make and loved by everyone.

[Serves 2]

300ml (10fl oz) milk
a few drops vanilla essence
pinch cinnamon powder
4 slices slightly stale bread
2 eggs, lightly beaten
30g (1oz) butter
icing sugar
strawberries

Warm the milk, vanilla essence and cinnamon powder in a saucepan. Take one slice of bread and dip it in the milk and then in the beaten egg. Melt the butter in a frying pan and fry the dipped bread for 1 minute on each side, until golden and crispy. Drain on kitchen paper.

Serve hot, dusted with icing sugar and garnished with strawberries.

An Old-time Egg and Fish Pie

This pie was one of my dear Aunt Audrey's favourite recipes and was very popular with her many welcome callers. Although I have given this pie a more unusual topping of deep-fried vegetable crisps, the traditional potato topping will work equally well if you are pressed for time. Alternatively, make the vegetable crisps in advance and store in an airtight tin until you need them.

[Serves 6-8]

500g (1lb) smoked fish, cubed
500g (1lb) white fish (cod, haddock or whiting), cubed
50g (1½oz) butter or margarine
50g (1½oz) flour
1l (1½pt) milk
1 egg yolk
120g (4oz) frozen peas
salt and pepper
pinch paprika
6 hard-boiled eggs, quartered

TOPPING
1 potato
1 parsnip
1 yam or potato
1 beetroot
oil to deep fry
1 tsp onion salt
½ tsp chilli powder

Preheat oven to gas mark 5, 375°F, 190°C. Place the cubes of fish in a well-greased, oven-proof dish and set aside.

To make the crispy topping: slice the vegetables very finely. Blanch the potato, parsnip and yam in boiling water for 30 seconds. Then drain, pat dry, and slice finely. Deep-fry each vegetable separately to preserve individual flavours. The beetroot does not require blanching before being deep-fried, but ensure that it has been cooked and peeled before slicing. As the vegetable slices are removed from the fat, drain on kitchen paper and then sprinkle with onion salt and chilli powder. Keep warm while the pie is prepared.

Melt the butter in a saucepan and add the flour, milk and egg yolk, mixing well to prevent lumps. Bring slowly to the boil. Add the peas and the seasonings and cook for 1 minute, then add the boiled eggs. Pour the sauce over the fish, cover the dish with foil and bake in the oven for 25 minutes. Make sure the fish is cooked through before removing from the oven. Top the pie with vegetable crisps or mashed potato.

Peppered Bacon and Eggs

A novel way to serve these popular breakfast ingredients at lunch time or as a snack.

[Serves 6]

3 peppers, red, green or yellow
6 rashers of bacon, back or streaky
6 eggs (size 3)
6 tsp olive oil
black pepper
30g (1oz) breadcrumbs
30g (1oz) grated cheese (optional)
300ml (10fl oz) vegetable stock

TO SERVE
2 dsp parsley, finely chopped
toast

Preheat oven to gas mark 5, 375°F, 190°C. Cut the peppers in half, de-seed and place in an ovenproof dish. Put 1 rasher of bacon and crack 1 egg into each pepper half. Spoon over a little olive oil. Season with black pepper and sprinkle with breadcrumbs and cheese. Pour stock around the peppers, cover with foil, and bake in the oven for at least 25 minutes (the cooking time will depend on the size of the peppers and the thickness of the bacon.)

When ready, sprinkle with parsley and serve hot with toast.

Tasty Family Omelette

For a good tasty omelette use the freshest of eggs and be careful not to overbeat them. The topping can be varied according to what is in season and personal taste.

[*Serves 2*]

6 eggs
3 tbsp water
salt and pepper
15g (½oz) butter

TOPPING
1 dsp oil
1 onion, finely chopped
4 rashers of bacon, chopped
60g (2oz) mushrooms, sliced
1 red pepper, chopped
1 green pepper, chopped
1 potato, boiled and sliced
2 tsp spring onions, finely chopped

TO PREPARE THE TOPPING

Heat the oil in a frying pan and gently fry the onion, bacon, sliced mushrooms and chopped peppers for several minutes. Add the potato and the spring onions and heat thoroughly.

TO MAKE THE OMELETTE

Gently whisk the eggs with a fork for no more than 15 seconds. Then add the water and the seasoning and mix well. Melt the butter in a frying pan and when it is frothy and bubbling pour in the eggs. Shake the frying pan to ensure the egg is evenly spread. When the omelette is almost set, add the topping and finish off under the grill.

Soufflé Omelette

This type of omelette has a very different texture and is often served as a pudding. The main difference between a standard and a soufflé omelette is the way in which the eggs are beaten. In a soufflé omelette the eggs are separated and the whites are beaten separately before being folded into the egg yolks.

[Serves 1]

3 eggs, separated
1 dsp caster sugar
15g (½oz) butter
rind of 1 lemon

TO SERVE
15g (½oz) icing sugar
½ tsp lemon juice

Beat the eggs yolks and caster sugar together until creamy. In a separate bowl, whisk the egg whites until they form soft peaks. Then fold the egg whites into the whisked yolks. Heat the butter in a frying pan and when frothy pour in the egg mixture and sprinkle with lemon rind. Cook for one minute then transfer the pan to the grill and continue cooking until the omelette rises and is golden.

Serve dusted with icing sugar and sprinkled with lemon juice.

A Freezing
Hot Pudding

This pudding is always very popular, especially with children who find the idea of cooking ice cream in the oven quite intriguing! I have used strawberries and kiwi fruit but any fruit can be used. Don't worry if you don't have the time to bake a sponge cake, a bought one will suffice, or you can even use trifle sponges.

[Serves 6-8]

STRAWBERRY PURÉE
8 strawberries
30g (1oz) icing sugar

ICE CREAM LAYER CAKE
2 sponge rectangles, 2cm (1 inch) in thickness,
(cut to the same size as the ice cream block)
250g (8oz) fresh strawberries, sliced
3 kiwi fruit, peeled and sliced
1 block of vanilla ice cream

MERINGUE
4 egg whites
250g (8oz) caster sugar
caster sugar and flaked almonds for sprinkling

To make the purée, press the strawberries through a sieve to form a pulp. Add the icing sugar and mix well.

Place one of the sponge layers on a baking sheet and spread with half of the puree and arrange half of the strawberries and kiwi fruit on top. Place the block of ice cream on top of the fruit, followed by the second sponge layer. Spread the sponge with the remaining strawberry purée and top with the rest of the fruit. Place in the freezer to keep firm while the meringue is prepared.

Preheat oven to gas mark 8, 450°F, 220°C. Beat together the egg whites and half the sugar until very stiff and forming peaks. Fold in the remaining sugar and mix well. Spread the meringue over the ice cream cake, ensuring that it is completely covered on all sides. Sprinkle a little caster sugar and flaked almonds over the top and bake for 5-6 minutes until the meringue is golden and cooked. Serve at once, decorated with sliced strawberries.

Tasty Family Omelette

One-mix
Victoria Sponge Cake

This all-in-one cake mixture works extremely well, resulting in a beautifully textured cake. The subtle lemon flavour combines well with good old-fashioned lemon curd (see p. 53). The addition of the baking powder ensures that the cake rises and is light in texture.

250g (8oz) butter or margarine
250g (8oz) caster sugar
250g (8oz) self-raising flour, sieved
1 tsp baking powder
4 eggs, lightly beaten
rind ½ lemon, finely grated
1 dsp water (if necessary)
strawberry jam or lemon curd

Preheat oven to gas mark 3, 325°F, 160°C. Grease two 20cm (8 inch) sponge tins and line with greaseproof paper.

Put the butter, sugar, sieved flour, baking powder, eggs and lemon rind into a large bowl. Mix together well, either by hand or using an electric mixer, until smooth and creamy. If the mixture appears a little stiff add 1 dsp water before transferring the mixture to the cake tins. Bake for 30 minutes or until golden and firm to the touch. Turn out on to a cooling tray.

When cold spread one side of each with a little strawberry jam or lemon curd and sandwich together.

Old-fashioned Lemon Curd

This lemon curd will keep in an airtight jar for up to two weeks, if stored in the fridge.

3 egg yolks
125g (4oz) caster sugar
50g (1½oz) butter, diced
juice of 1 large lemon
rind of ½ lemon

Put the egg yolks and caster sugar into a heat resistant bowl and whisk together until light and creamy. Place the bowl over a saucepan of gently boiling water and slowly add the diced butter, whisking continuously. When the butter has melted, gradually add the lemon juice and rind, mixing well all the while. Continue beating until the mixture thickens. Allow to cool before pouring into an airtight, sterilised jar.

Overleaf: Victoria Sponge Cake and Lemon Curd (left) and Irish Whiskey Syllabub (right)

Irish Whiskey Syllabub

The flavour of the whiskey combines well with the tangy lemon in this delicate, light pudding.

[Serves 4-6]

1 tbsp lemon juice
rind of 1 lemon, finely grated
60g (2oz) caster sugar
8 tbsp Irish whiskey
300ml (10fl oz) double cream
1 egg white, whisked

Put the lemon juice, lemon rind, sugar and whiskey into a mixing bowl and beat until the sugar is dissolved. In a separate bowl, whisk the cream until it forms soft peaks and then add to the whiskey and lemon mixture. Fold in the whisked egg white. Transfer the mixture into tall glasses and chill in the fridge for 1 hour.

Serve sprinkled with finely grated lemon rind.

4

A Good Roasting

Roasting , as far as I am concerned, is one of the most relaxed and trouble-free ways of cooking. It gives flavour, aroma, and texture whether you are oven-roasting pork, pot-roasting beef, open-roasting fish, or cooking an assortment of fruit and vegetables for starters and puddings.

Recipes

· *A Pepper-crusted Loin of Pork*

· *Pumpkin with Garlic and Honey*

· *Spare Ribs with a Hot Spicy Sauce*

· *Peaches with an Aromatic Topping*

· *Spiced Lamb Chops with Crispy Potatoes and Roasted Red Onions*

· *Family Pot Roast*

· *Roasted Butternut Squash Au Gratin*

· *Oven-roasted Courgettes*

· *Roasted Hake Steaks with Lime Butter Sauce*

· *Autumn Fruits in Amaretto Soufflé*

A Pepper-crusted Loin of Pork

Loin of pork has to be one of the most suitable cuts of pork for roasting. In this recipe I have replaced the crackling for what I feel is a tastier coating, although the crackling can still be cooked separately.

[Serves 8-10]

1 loin of pork (approximately 5lb)

PEPPER TOPPING
30g (1oz) red peppercorns
30g (1oz) green peppercorns
30g (1oz) black peppercorns
60g (2oz) wholemeal breadcrumbs
1 tsp dry mustard
2 dsp parsley, finely chopped
4 dsp honey
1 dsp olive oil

TO COOK
30g (1oz) butter
2 dsp olive oil
150ml (5fl oz) dry cider

Preheat oven to gas mark 7, 425°F, 220°C. To prepare the loin first remove the skin and most of the fat from the pork (if you intend making crackling, try to remove the fat in one piece).

Crush the peppercorns coarsely and mix with the breadcrumbs, mustard, parsley, half the honey and olive oil or butter. Mix together well. Spread the remaining honey over the pork and then sprinkle on the peppercorn mixture and pat down well. I usually reserve a little of the coating mixture to spread over the loin about 30 minutes before serving as it I think it looks more attractive. Pour oil and butter around the joint, then place it in the oven to roast for 45 minutes. Then pour the cider around the joint and return it to the oven for 1½ hours.

To test if the pork is cooked, insert a skewer into the joint; if the juices run clear then the meat is ready. When cooked, leave the pork in a warm place to relax for 15 minutes. This will allow the juices to return to the meat making it more tender.

If cooking crackling, score the skin and fat removed from the loin. Sprinkle

with salt and roast at the top of the oven for 30 minutes until very crispy. Serve with the pork.

Pumpkin with Garlic and Honey

This recipe calls for pumpkin, but this is an equally tasty way to cook any assortment of winter squashes; pumpkin, butternut or spaghetti. All cook best by roasting, as this allows their flavour to develop without them drowning in water.

[Serves 6]

4 dsp oil
4 dsp honey
4 cloves garlic
black pepper
750g (1½lb) pumpkin, peeled and cut into 2cm (1 inch) cubes

Preheat oven to gas mark 5, 375°F, 190°C. Heat the oil in a roasting dish, together with the honey, garlic and pepper. Add the pumpkin cubes and toss well to ensure all the flesh is coated. Roast in the oven for 45 minutes. I prefer not to cover the pumpkin when it is in the oven, as I find the roasting process gives it a lovely crispy texture and golden colour.

Spare Ribs with a Hot Spicy Sauce

Pork spare ribs are always popular and one of the best ways to cook them is to roast them in the oven with a spicy marinade.

[Serves 6]

1 dsp oil
2 cloves garlic, very finely chopped
2cm- (1 inch-) cube of root ginger, very finely chopped
1 tsp dried mustard
1 tsp tomato puree
1 dsp wine vinegar
1 dsp chilli sauce
2 dsp honey
4 dsp soy sauce
4 dsp soft brown sugar
150ml (5fl oz) water or beef stock
750g (1½lb) pork spare ribs

Preheat oven to gas mark 5, 375°F, 190°C. Heat the oil in a saucepan and then add all the other ingredients. Stir well and bring to a boil for 5 minutes before pouring the sauce over the pork ribs. Toss well, ensuring they are well coated before roasting in the oven for 1 hour until well cooked and crispy.

Serve hot.

Overleaf: Spare Ribs (left) and Peaches with an Aromatic Topping (right)

Peaches with an Aromatic Topping

These tasty little peaches go particularly well with pork. The nutty, savoury topping can be gently spiced with cloves or nutmeg to enhance the flavour. Substitute the peaches with apples, if you like: the topping works equally well with both.

[*Serves 6*]

SUGAR SYRUP
300ml (10fl oz) water
30g (1oz) granulated sugar
2 cinnamon sticks

PEACHES WITH AN AROMATIC TOPPING
5 peaches, stoned and cut in half (tinned peaches can be used)
30g (1oz) wholemeal breadcrumbs
30g (1oz) soft brown sugar
30g (1oz) pistachio nuts or walnuts, chopped
30g (1oz) almonds, chopped
1 egg yolk
1 dsp parsley
1 dsp sugar syrup

Make the sugar syrup by boiling the water, granulated sugar and cinnamon sticks together for 1 minute. Remove from heat and set aside.

Preheat oven to gas mark 5, 375°F, 190°C. Place the peach halves in an ovenproof dish and pour the sugar syrup over them. Add one of the cinnamon sticks to the syrup.

Mix together the breadcrumbs, brown sugar, nuts, egg yolk, parsley and 1 dsp sugar syrup into a bowl . Spoon a little of the mixture on to the top of each peach and then place in the oven for 20 minutes.

Spiced Lamb Chops with Crispy Potatoes and Roasted Red Onions

This spicy dish combines a complete meal in a foil parcel which is then roasted. Choose chops that are no more than 1cm (½ inch) thick and allow them to marinate in the orange juice for at least 15 minutes before cooking.

[Serves 3]

3 lamb chops
juice and rind of 1 orange
1 tsp tomato puree
1½ tsp cajun spice
1 dsp olive oil
2 red onions, thickly sliced
3 potatoes, thickly sliced
300ml (10fl oz) vegetable or beef stock
1 dsp lemon juice
2 dsp parsley, finely chopped

Place each lamb chop on a square of silver foil and seal each end securely, but leave the top open. Divide the orange juice, rind and tomato puree evenly between the three parcels. Sprinkle each chop with a little Cajun spice; this will flavour and colour the meat.

Heat the oil in a frying pan and fry the onions and potatoes until crispy and golden. Spoon the onions and potatoes over the chops, pour over a little stock and the lemon juice (this will keep the potatoes a good colour). Seal the top of the foil parcel and roast in the oven at gas mark 5, 375°F, 190°F, for 1 hour. Open the parcels and return to the oven for a further 15 minutes or until the lamb is crispy and golden.

Sprinkle with parsley and serve hot.

Family Pot Roast

This traditional pot roast can be made with topside, silverside or, the one that I prefer, brisket. Whichever cut you choose, this is one of the best ways to tenderise the more economical cuts of meat.

[Serves 8]

1 dsp oil
1 dsp butter
rolled brisket (approx. 5lb)
3 large onions
2 carrots, roughly chopped
2 parsnips, roughly chopped
250g (8oz) small potatoes, peeled
2 leeks, roughly chopped
600ml (1pt) water or stock
1 dsp parsley
30g (1oz) plain flour
4 dsp warm water
few drops of Worcestershire sauce

Heat the oil and butter in a large heavy-based saucepan. Add the meat and onions and toss well in the oil to seal in the meat juices and give the meat a golden coating. Allow time for this step to ensure that the meat is evenly browned without it blackening. Add the carrots and parsnips. The potatoes and leeks can also be added at this point but the colour will be much improved if they are cooked separately, incorporated just before serving and then heated through. Add the seasoning and the water or stock and cook on a low simmering heat until the meat is tender and cooked. Cooking time for this type of meat is difficult to judge, but a 5lb brisket will take at least 3 hours. The meat juices can be thickened and served as a gravy by adding 1oz of flour blended with warm water and a few drops of Worcestershire sauce just before the dish is served.

Serve hot, garnished with parsley.

Roasted Butternut Squash Au Gratin

Squashes cook best by being roasted in the oven. The butternut squash has a dense texture, and also has the ability to absorb the flavour of whatever it is being cooked with.

[*Serves 2*]

1 small butternut squash
30g (1oz) wholemeal breadcrumbs
1 tomato, skinned and chopped
30g (1oz) Parmesan cheese
1 dsp olive oil
black pepper
1 dsp parsley

Preheat oven to gas mark 6, 400°F, 200°C. Roast the whole squash on a baking sheet for 30 minutes until it shows signs of softening. Cut in half, remove the seeds, scoop out about one-third of the flesh, and return to the baking sheet.

Mix together the breadcrumbs, tomato, two-thirds of the Parmesan cheese, olive oil, pepper and parsley and then spoon this mixture back into the squash. Sprinkle the remaining cheese on top and roast in the oven for 15-20 minutes until melted and golden.

Serve hot.

Oven-roasted Courgettes with Olives

This vegetable dish is particularly good with fish. Be careful not to overcook the courgettes or they will lose their texture.

[Serves 4]

4 courgettes
12 olives
2 dsp oil
black pepper

Preheat oven to gas mark 6, 400°F, 200°C. Slice the courgettes thickly, lengthways, and place in an ovenproof dish with the olives, oil and black pepper. Cook uncovered, turning occasionally, for 15 minutes.

Overleaf: Courgettes with Olives (left) and Roasted Hake Steaks (right)

Roasted Hake Steaks with Lime Butter Sauce

This tasty dish of hake steaks shows how well fish roasts in the oven. Remember to remove the foil for the last 10 minutes of the cooking time in order to develop the texture and appearance of the fish. This trouble-free recipe is also a good way to serve salmon steaks.

[Serves 4]

2 fennel bulbs, roughly chopped
bunch of thyme
peel of 1 lemon, roughly chopped
300ml (10fl oz) water
4 dsp dry vermouth or white wine
black pepper
30g butter
1 tsp lemon juice
1 tsp lime juice
4 hake steaks, 3cm (1½ inch) thick

Preheat oven to gas mark 6, 400°F, 200°C. Place the fennel, thyme, lemon peel, water, vermouth or white wine, and the seasoning in an ovenproof dish.

Prepare the lime butter by mixing the butter, lemon and lime juice. Coat the steaks well on both sides with the butter. Place on top of the bed of fennel and cover with foil. Bake in the oven for 35 minutes, turning once. Remove the foil from the fish and return to the oven for a further 10 minutes so that the fish becomes crispy and brown. Serve hot.

Autumn Fruits in an Amaretto Soufflé

This is a rather clever soufflé which holds better than any other soufflé recipe that I know. It is delicately flavoured with Amaretto liqueur, and a variety of fruits can be used: try apples, plums, pears or a selection of seasonal berries. Great care is needed when folding in the egg whites if the soufflé is to stay light and fluffy.

[Serves 6]

6 apples, cored
6 plums, stones removed
30g (1oz) demerara sugar
150ml (5fl oz) maple syrup or honey
50g (1½oz) plain flour
30g (1oz) butter (cold and firm)
30g (1oz) almonds, ground
60g (2oz) caster sugar
200ml (7fl oz) milk
3 dsp Amaretto liqueur
4 eggs, separated
30g (1oz) almonds, flaked

Preheat oven to gas mark 6, 400°F, 200°C and lightly grease a large ovenproof dish.

Put the fruit into the dish, sprinkle with demerara sugar and pour over the maple syrup or honey. Roast in the oven for 15-20 minutes until slightly softened.

Mix together the flour, butter, ground almonds and caster sugar in a food processor until the mixture resembles breadcrumbs. Heat the milk in a saucepan and slowly add the crumble mixture whisking all the time until the milk comes to the boil. Pour into a bowl and, when cool, add the Amaretto and mix well. Lightly beat the egg yolks and then whisk into the mixture one at a time. In a separate bowl, whisk the egg whites until they form soft peaks, and then carefully fold into the mixture. Pour this over the roasted fruits, sprinkle with almonds and place in the oven for 20 minutes until the soufflé has risen and is firm.

Serve at once with lightly whipped cream flavoured with nutmeg.

5

Going with the Grain

Aren't grains just great! We used to think that cereals, seeds and grains were a very basic food, but now we have come to appreciate how good and healthy they are. Use them to make perfect puddings, ravishing risottos, splendid stews or even home-baked bread.

Recipes

· *Sunshine Sultana Soda Bread*

· *Aromatic Rice*

· *Gypsy Stew*

· *Outrageous Raisin and Rye Gingerbread*

· *A Golden-grained Risotto*

· *Apple Pie in a Pot*

· *Fingerprint Bread*

· *Marmalade Muffins*

· *Oat 'n' Apple Cake*

· *Irish Meadow Honey Biscuits*

· *Lemon Barley Water*

Sunshine Sultana Soda Bread

This is one of my favourite traditional Irish breads. It is simple to make, especially when you use the convenient soda bread self-raising flour, which does not require the addition of a separate raising agent. The amount of buttermilk required depends on the brand of flour you use, so add it gradually until it is the consistency you need.

500g (1lb) soda bread self-raising flour
1 tsp salt
30g (1oz) caster sugar
60g (2oz) butter or margarine
60g (2oz) golden sultanas
300-450ml (10-15fl oz) buttermilk

Preheat oven to gas mark 6, 400°F, 200°C. Sieve the flour and salt into a bowl, add the sugar and rub in the butter or margarine. Stir in the sultanas. Make a well in the centre of the mixture and add the buttermilk. Mix to a soft but firm dough, turn out on to a floured table and knead gently. Shape into a round, mark a cross on the top with a sharp knife. Place on a floured baking sheet and bake in the oven for 20-25 minutes.

Previous page: Sunshine Sultana Soda Bread

Aromatic
Rice

This gently-scented aromatic rice dish is made with fine quality basmati rice which has a superb flavour. The preparation of the caramelised peel is time consuming but I feel that it is well worth the effort.

[Serves 4]

CARAMELISED PEEL
5 each oranges, lemons, limes, clementines
water for boiling
500g (1lb) granulated sugar

AROMATIC RICE
½ tsp salt
1½l (2½ pt) chicken stock
500g (1lb) basmati rice
a few strands of saffron soaked in 2 dsp warm water
60g (2oz) almonds, toasted and sliced
60g (2oz) pistachio nuts, sliced
2 dsp orange caramelised peel
1 dsp each lime, lemon, clementine caramelised peel

TO MAKE THE CARAMELISED PEEL
It is important that each variety of fruit peel is made as a different batch to retain individual flavours. Remove the peel from the fruits using a sharp knife, being careful not to remove any of the bitter, white pith. Cut the peel into very fine strands and place in a saucepan. Cover with water and bring to the boil. Change the water and bring to the boil again. Change the water a third time, add 125g (4oz) sugar and bring to the boil. Cook for at least 5 minutes until the syrup shows signs of thickening. Allow to cool before bottling the peel and syrup in sterile airtight jars. The peel should keep for 1-2 weeks. Repeat until all fruit has been caramelised.

TO COOK THE AROMATIC RICE
Add the salt to the stock and bring to a boil. Add rice and stir once. Boil gently for 10-12 minutes. Remove from the boil (the rice should not require draining), and add the saffron, nuts, peel and 4 dsp peel syrup to the rice and serve hot.

Gypsy Stew

This tender lamb stew combines grains, pulses and a crunchy oatmeal topping together to create a healthy casserole.

[*Serves 6*]

125g (4oz) each green, red and brown lentils
125g (4oz) chick peas
1l (2pt) water
750g (1½lbs) lamb pieces
60g (2oz) fine oatmeal
3 dsp oil
2 cloves garlic, chopped
1 red onion, sliced
1 large tin tomatoes, chopped
500ml (1 pt) water or stock
1 tsp turmeric powder
1 tsp cinnamon powder
salt and pepper

TOPPING
60g (2oz) butter or margarine
125g (4oz) pin head oatmeal
60g (2oz) hazelnuts or pine nuts
pinch parsley or rosemary, chopped

Soak the lentils and chick peas in the water for an hour.

Preheat oven to gas mark 5, 375°F, 190°C. Toss the lamb pieces in oatmeal, and brown in a frying pan in 2 dsp of hot oil for several minutes until golden and crispy. Place in a casserole dish. In a separate pan, heat the remaining oil and fry the garlic and onion until softened and then pour on top of the lamb. Add the drained pulses, the tomatoes, water or stock, turmeric, cinnamon and salt and pepper. Put the casserole dish into the oven and cook for 45 minutes.

To make the topping, melt the butter or margarine in a saucepan, add the oatmeal, nuts and parsley or rosemary, and toss for several minutes. Sprinkle on top of the casserole, then return the dish to the oven for a further 15-20 minutes until the meat is tender and the topping is crunchy.

Outrageous Raisin and Rye Gingerbread

There are hundreds of varieties of gingerbread but this is one of my favourites. The rye flakes add a unique texture to the bread. A novel serving idea for a quick and simple pudding is to slice the gingerbread very thinly, fry the slices in butter, and serve with poached peaches and yoghurt.

180g (6oz) plain flour
60g (2oz) rye flakes
1 tsp bicarbonate of soda
1 tsp ginger powder
1 tsp cinnamon powder
125g (4oz) butter or margarine
125g (4oz) soft brown sugar
1 dsp treacle
1 dsp honey
120g (4oz) raisins
50ml (2fl oz) milk
1 egg (size 1), lightly beaten

Preheat oven to gas mark 4, 350°F, 180°C. Grease and line a 2lb loaf tin. Sieve the flour into a bowl, add the rye flakes, bicarbonate of soda, ginger and cinnamon, and mix well. Melt the butter in a saucepan, then add the sugar, treacle, honey and raisins, and mix well before adding the milk. Allow to cool slightly before adding to the flour mixture. Stir well. Add the beaten egg and mix well. Transfer to the loaf tin. Bake for 1 hour or until firm and golden.

A Golden-grained Risotto

The quality of stock you use is equally as important as the choice of grain for a risotto. I have used a whole-grain rice for texture, colour and flavour but the traditional arborio rice can also be used.

[Serves 6]

3 dsp oil
500g (1lb) whole-grain rice
½ tsp salt
1l (2 pt) chicken stock
3 chicken fillets
1 tsp turmeric powder
1 tsp paprika
½ tsp onion salt
2 tsp coarsely ground black pepper
2 yellow peppers, quartered and de-seeded
2 oranges or peaches, cut into segments

SAUCE
150ml (5fl oz) cream
1 tsp whole-grain mustard
pinch paprika
2 dsp spring onion, chopped
1 dsp orange juice (optional)

Heat 1 dsp oil in a large saucepan, add the rice and stir until completely coated. In a separate saucepan, heat the seasoned stock until boiling. Then pour over the rice and boil for 10-12 minutes until the stock has been absorbed and the grains of rice are tender.

While the rice is cooking, prepare the chicken. Brush the fillets with the remaining oil and dust with the turmeric, paprika, onion salt and black pepper. Fry in oil for 5 minutes, turning once. Transfer to under a grill and cook for a further 7-8 minutes until chargrilled and well cooked. Cut each fillet into 3 or 4 strips and set aside. Grill the peppers for 3-4 minutes and add to the rice together with the orange or peach segments and the chicken strips. Toss thoroughly. Mix together the cream, mustard, paprika, spring onions and orange juice, and pour over the risotto. Heat thoroughly in a saucepan and serve garnished with spring onions and grated orange rind.

Overleaf: Golden-grained Risotto (left) and Apple Pie (right)

Apple Pie in a Pot

This recipe is one of my favourite ways of making apple pie. There is no need to roll out pastry, simply flatten the dough into rounds with your hands and use this to cover the apples.

[*Serves 8*]

FILLING
1kg (2lb) Bramley apples, peeled, cored and sliced
2 dsp water
1 dsp lemon juice
30g (1oz) caster sugar
pinch cinnamon or cloves, ground

PASTRY
180g (6oz) butter or margarine
180g (6oz) caster sugar
2 eggs (size 3), lightly beaten
300g (10oz) self-raising flour
Icing or caster sugar to dust

Preheat the oven to gas mark 5, 375°F, 190°C. Poach the apples gently in 2 dsp water and 1 dsp of lemon juice. Add sugar and spice to taste. Leave to cool.

Put the butter or margarine and the sugar into a saucepan and heat gently until melted. Allow to cool. Add the lightly beaten eggs and the sieved flour and bind the mixture into a soft dough. While the dough is still warm press two-thirds of it into the base of a greased 22cm (9 inch) pie dish. Spoon the cooled apples over the top. Shape the remaining pastry into 5 or 6 flattened rounds and arrange on top of the apples, ensuring the filling is well covered. Bake for 25 minutes until golden brown.

Serve warm, dusted with icing or caster sugar

Fingerprint Bread

A novel way of decorating home-baked bread. Simply stick your finger into it after the final proving and before baking in the oven. I like the unusual effect it gives.

550g (1lb 2oz) strong plain flour
1 tsp salt
½ tsp baking powder
50g (1½oz) butter or margarine
2 sachets Easy-Blend yeast
300ml (10fl oz) tepid water
1 egg, beaten

Put the flour, salt, baking powder and butter into a food processor and mix pulse until the butter has been blended into the dry ingredients. Sprinkle the dried yeast on top of the flour and add the water gradually to mix to a soft elastic dough. Knead on a floured surface for 8-10 minutes. Place in a greased bowl, cover with plastic film and leave to prove for 20-25 minutes or until the dough has doubled in size.

Preheat oven to gas mark 6, 400°F, 200°C. Knead the dough again for 4-5 minutes to disperse the strong smell of yeast. Divide the dough into two, shape each into a round. Place on a floured baking tray and set aside for 15-20 minutes to prove a second time. Decorate with fingerprints, brush with beaten egg and bake in the oven for 25 minutes.

When cooked, the bread will sound hollow when tapped underneath. Remove from oven, wrap in a clean tea towel and leave to cool.

Marmalade Muffins

This recipe is made using baking powder and gluten-free flour, a very soft flour with a distinctive texture, designed for people with intolerance to the protein gluten. This basic recipe can be turned into savoury muffins by substituting the marmalade and sugar with 1 tsp chopped herbs, 2 dsp onions and 60g (2oz) grated cheese.

[Makes 12]

300g (10oz) gluten-free flour
1 tsp gluten-free baking powder
1 dsp caster sugar
pinch salt
2 dsp coarse marmalade
100g (3oz) butter or margarine, softened
1 egg, lightly beaten
150ml (5fl oz) milk
30g (1oz) walnuts, chopped

Preheat the oven to gas mark 4, 350°F, 180°C, and grease 12 muffins tins. Sieve the flour and baking powder into a bowl. then add the sugar and salt. Add the marmalade, softened butter, egg and milk, and mix to a smooth dough (the consistency will be softer than a dough made with ordinary flour). Pour into the muffin tins, sprinkle with the walnuts and bake for 20-25 minutes.

Oat 'n' Apple Cake

Jumbo oats are used in this recipe both as a base and a topping for this delicious and light apple cake. I have added a little honey to the oats and butter base as I find it gives better results when it comes to serving the cake in slices.

[Serves 8]

BASE
1 dsp honey
50g (1½oz) butter or margarine
½ tsp cinnamon
160g (5oz) jumbo oats

FILLING
1kg (2lb) Bramley apples, peeled, cored and sliced
30g (1oz) caster sugar
1 dsp lemon juice
15g (½oz) gelatine
4 dsp water
6 dsp concentrated apple juice
4 dsp Calvados liqueur
300ml (10fl oz) whipping cream or yoghurt
few drops of green colouring
pinch cinnamon (optional)

Melt the honey and butter in a saucepan, add the cinnamon and 100g (3oz) oats and cook for 2-3 minutes until crispy and golden. Then pack firmly into a well-greased, 20cm (8 inch), loose-bottomed cake tin.

Prepare the filling by poaching the apple slices in water, sugar and lemon juice for 8-10 minutes over a gentle heat. Then puree or mash with a fork. Put the gelatine and water into a heat-resistant bowl. Place over a saucepan of boiling water and stir until the gelatine has dissolved, being careful not to overheat. Add the concentrated apple juice, 2 dsp Calvados and the dissolved gelatine to the apple puree. Leave to cool, then add the whipped cream, a little green colouring and the cinnamon. Mix gently then pour over the oat base and chill in the fridge for 1½-2 hours. Mix the remaining jumbo oats and Calvados together and brown under a grill before sprinkling on top of the cake. Decorate with fresh apple slices.

Irish Meadow Honey Biscuits

The delicious taste of honey and the crunchy texture of these biscuits make them popular with everyone. They can be stored in an airtight container but they disappear so quickly that there are seldom any left!

[Makes 12]

125g (4oz) butter
60g (2oz) caster sugar
4 tbsp meadow honey
1 egg yolk
30g (1oz) cornflakes
150g (5oz) plain flour, sieved

Preheat the oven to gas mark 4, 350°F, 180°C. Beat together the butter and caster sugar until light and creamy. Fold in the honey, egg yolk and cornflakes. Gradually add the sieved plain flour and mix to a stiff dough. Turn on to a lightly floured surface and roll to 1.2cm (1.4 inch) thickness. Cut into biscuit shapes with a pastry cutter. Place on a lightly greased baking tray and bake for 10-15 minutes until firm and golden.

Remove from the baking tray and allow to cool on a wire rack. Store in an airtight container.

Overleaf: Meadow Honey Biscuits (left) and Lemon Barley Water (right)

Lemon Barley Water

I find the flavour of pearl barley water dull and insipid, yet when you combine it with tangy lemon, you have a soothing, refreshing drink that has been popular for generations. The cooked pearl barley itself can be reheated and used in a variety of ways. It is ideal for a risotto (see p. 81).

4 lemons
150g (5oz) granulated sugar
½ tsp nutmeg (optional)
250g (4oz) pearl barley
2l (4pt) cold water

Squeeze the juice from the lemons and coarsely cut off the peel, being careful not to remove the white pith as this causes the barley water to develop a bitter flavour. Place the peel, sugar, nutmeg and 250ml (½ pt) of water in a saucepan and bring to a boil. Simmer for 15 minutes until the lemon flavour develops. Leave to cool and then remove the peel. Add the lemon juice to the saucepan and stir.

In a separate saucepan cover the pearl barley with cold water and bring to a boil. Allow to cool before draining and discarding the water. Rinse the barley under cold running water to remove any scum. Return to the saucepan with the 2l (4 pt) water. Bring to a boil and simmer very gently for 15-10 minutes. Strain off the barley water and mix with the lemon syrup. Chill in the fridge.

This is a drink, not a cordial, but if you like you can dilute it a little with sparkling water.

6
Perfecting the Pasta

I t's only in recent years that we have come to appreciate what Italians have known for generations – that pasta is one of the most delicious foods: quick to prepare, cheap and very healthy.

Recipes
· *Chicken Tagliatelle with a Sweet Pepper Sauce*
· *Home-made Pasta with a Simple Mushroom Sauce*
· *Five-minute Pasta*
· *Quick and Easy Pasta*
· *Cannelloni with Parma Ham and Cheese*
· *Home-made Sun-dried Tomatoes*
· *Lamb Meatballs with Pasta and Sun-dried Tomato Sauce*
· *Pasta with Scallops*

Chicken Tagliatelle with a Sweet Pepper Sauce

The combination of plain and green pasta together with the peppers make this a very colourful dish, ideal for a buffet. Any colour of peppers can be used, but I prefer the flavour of the sweeter yellow peppers for the sauce.

[Serves 6]

3 yellow peppers, halved
2 green or red peppers, de-seeded and chopped
4 dsp white wine
2 dsp grapeseed oil
750g (1½lb) chicken fillets, sliced
250g (8oz) mushrooms, sliced
1 green or yellow courgette, sliced
12 olives, black or green
salt and pepper
2l (3 pt) water
½ tsp salt
1 dsp oil
500g (1lb) tagliatelle, plain and green
parsley or tarragon, chopped

To make the sauce: roast the yellow peppers in the oven for 15 minutes or until almost chargrilled and soft. Remove the skins and purée in a blender, then add the wine and mix well.

Heat the grapeseed oil in a large frying pan or wok and add the sliced chicken. Stir-fry until light gold and almost cooked, then add the green or red peppers, mushrooms, courgette and stir-fry again for 4 minutes. Add the olives and mix well. Pour the pepper sauce over the chicken and vegetables and season to taste. Keep warm.

Boil the water in a large pot, add the salt and oil, then the tagliatelle. Cook for 10 minutes then drain. Add the chicken and sauce mixture and toss to coat the pasta.

Serve hot with a garnish of chopped tarragon or parsley.

Home-made Pasta with a Simple Mushroom Sauce

Home-made pasta is so easy to make. It uses very simple ingredients, and the time needed to cook it is much shorter than commercially-made pasta. It should, however, be allowed to dry out for at least 10 minutes before being cooked. This mushroom sauce is delicious and very easy to make. I prefer to use cream in this recipe, but fromage frais is a virtually fat-free alternative for the calorie conscious.

[Serves 4]

PASTA
300g (10oz) plain flour
½ tsp salt
3 eggs
3 tsp olive oil
2½l (4 pt) water
½ tsp salt

MUSHROOM SAUCE
30g (1oz) butter or margarine
1 dsp olive oil
375g (12oz) assorted fresh mushrooms (button, oyster, shiitake)
2 spring onions, very finely chopped
1 tsp wholegrain mustard
150ml (5fl oz) whipping cream or fromage frais
salt and pepper
60g (2oz) Gruyere cheese, grated

Place the flour, salt, eggs and 2 dsp of the olive oil in a food processor and blend all the ingredients together. Turn the dough out on to a floured work surface and knead until it is smooth and elastic. Put the dough in a plastic bag and place in the fridge for at least 30 minutes. Then either put the dough through a pasta machine several times until the dough becomes fine, or roll out on a floured board until thin. Then cut into strips and leave to dry for ten minutes.

To cook the pasta fill a large saucepan with the water and bring to the boil. Add the salt and the remaining olive oil, then the pasta. Keep the water boiling rapidly and stir once or twice. The pasta is cooked when it floats to the top of the water. Be careful not to overcook; properly cooked, *al dente* pasta should retain a little bit of bite.

MUSHROOM SAUCE

Melt the butter or margarine in a large saucepan, then add the olive oil and mushrooms. (If using oyster mushrooms, keep these to the end as they require very little cooking.) Add the spring onions, mustard, cream or fromage frais and the seasoning. Be careful not to overheat as this will make the sauce thin. However, should this happen, simply mix ½oz cornflour with a little cream and add this to the sauce. Add the cheese, and serve the sauce hot poured over the drained pasta.

Five-Minute Pasta

This simple dish can be prepared very quickly using pasta, a packet sauce and smoked fish. It can even be microwaved to speed things up further.

[Serves 4-6]

2l (3 pt) water
½ tsp salt
1 dsp oil
250g (8oz) pasta spirals
500g (1lb) smoked whiting, cut into 2cm (1 inch) cubes
1 packet white sauce mix
300ml (10fl oz) milk
salt and pepper
1 dsp parsley, finely chopped
1 packet cheese and onion crisps, crushed

Boil the water in a large pot with the salt and oil, then add the pasta and cook for 5 minutes before draining. Place the whiting in a lightly greased ovenproof dish and pour the pasta on top.

Preheat oven to gas mark 6, 400°F, 200°C. Pour the sauce mix into a saucepan and gradually add the milk and seasoning, bring to the boil, stirring well, then add the parsley. Pour the sauce over the pasta, sprinkle with the crisps and bake in the oven for 25 minutes.

To check if the fish is cooked, press it with a fork; if it flakes apart easily it is cooked. Serve hot.

Quick and Easy Pasta

This dish makes use of a convenient bought tomato sauce, spiced up with Italian sausage. I am using farfalle or butterfly pasta which is very attractive.

[Serves 4]

2½l (4 pt) water
½ tsp salt
2 dsp oil
375g (12oz) farfalle
1 onion, finely chopped
250g (8oz) spicy Italian sausage, sliced finely
250g (8oz) jar pasta sauce
salt and pepper
½ tsp mixed dried herbs
250g (8oz) cannellini or fagiola beans, tinned
2 dsp red wine (optional)
fresh coriander or parsley, chopped

Put the water, salt and 1 dsp oil into a large saucepan and bring to a boil. Add the pasta and cook for 8 minutes or until *al dente*.

Heat the remaining oil in a large frying pan and fry the onion until softened but not browned, then add the Italian sausage and fry for 3 minutes. Add the pasta sauce and season to taste before adding the dried herbs, beans and red wine. Heat thoroughly.

To serve; drain the pasta and arrange on a heated platter, pour over the sauce and garnish with the chopped fresh herbs.

Quick and Easy Pasta

Cannelloni with Parma Ham and Cheese

This family-style, filling pasta dish combines spinach-flavoured pasta with Parma ham and soft cheese. It shows how easily home-made pasta can be prepared without the help of gadgets. If you have trouble rolling the dough wafer-thin, don't worry. Simply roll it out as thinly as you can manage, cut to size and then cook in oiled, boiling water for 2 minutes before draining.

[*Serves 6*]

SPINACH PASTA
60g (2oz) spinach, cooked and puréed
2 eggs, whisked
2 tbsp olive oil
½ tsp salt
250g (8oz) plain flour, sieved
1 egg, beaten

CHEESE FILLING
120g (4oz) Parma ham, sliced
250g (8oz) soft cheese, preferably ricotta
120g (4oz) spinach leaves, cooked
60g (2oz) wholemeal breadcrumbs
2 cloves garlic
1 egg

SAUCE
1 onion, finely chopped
60g (2oz) cooked ham or bacon, chopped
1 dsp oil
1 large can chopped tomatoes
dash worcestershire sauce
1 dsp basil, finely chopped
120g (4oz) Cheddar or Parmesan cheese, grated

Mix together the spinach purée, eggs, oil and salt in a mixing bowl, gradually add the flour and mix well. When the mixture forms a dough, turn it on to a floured work surface and knead for 10 minutes. Then place in a plastic bag and put in the fridge for 30 minutes to rest.

Roll out the dough until it is wafer-thin and cut into 6 sheets, 12cm x 8cm

(5 x 3 inch) in size. Leave flat on a table and brush with beaten egg.

To prepare the filling: heat the oil in a saucepan and fry the garlic for 2 minutes. Remove from the heat, add the breadcrumbs, spinach and egg, and mix well. Lay a piece of ham on each sheet of pasta, spread 1 dsp of filling on top and roll up to form a tube. Place in an ovenproof dish, join side down.

To make the sauce: heat the oil in a saucepan and fry the onion and bacon for 2 minutes, then add the tomatoes, basil and worcestershire sauce, and mix well. Spoon the sauce over the cannelloni tubes. (This dish needs plenty of sauce to ensure that the cannelloni tubes are moist and well cooked.) Sprinkle with grated cheese and bake in the oven for 30 minutes.

Home-made
Sun-dried Tomatoes

Although not a pasta dish, sun-dried tomatoes are so closely associated with pasta and other Italian-style dishes that this recipe seems most at home in this chapter. This novel way to make sun-dried tomatoes without the sunshine employs an oven at the lowest setting. These can be stored in olive oil in an airtight jar and can also be puréed in a blender and stored as sun-dried tomato paste.

1kg (2lb) small ripe tomatoes
sea salt
olive oil

TO STORE
olive oil to cover [approx. 300ml (10fl oz)]
1 tsp basil, parsley or oregaon, chopped

Cut the tomatoes in half and place, cut side up, on a baking sheet. Sprinkle with sea salt and olive oil and place in the oven (lowest setting) until the tomatoes have completely dried out. This will take approximately 14 hours and you should turn the tomatoes at least once during this time.

When dried pack into sterile jars and pour sufficient olive oil over the top to cover. Add 1 tsp of chopped herbs and seal with an airtight lid.

Overleaf: Sun-dried Tomatoes (left) and Lamb Meatballs with Pasta (right)

Lamb Meatballs with Pasta and Sun-dried Tomato Sauce

Minced lamb is becoming very popular and its delicate flavour combines well with spaghetti and a freshly-made tomato sauce. This sauce is used in many recipes and you can make it as spicy as you like.

[Serves 8]

500g (1lb) lean lamb, minced
1 onion, diced and fried in 1 dsp oil
4 fresh tomatoes, chopped
½ red chilli pepper, chopped
½ green chilli pepper, chopped
1 dsp chilli sauce
2 eggs, lightly beaten
1 dsp freshly chopped basil
120g (4oz) wholemeal breadcrumbs

SUN-DRIED TOMATO SAUCE
1 small onion, very finely chopped
2 cloves of garlic, finely chopped
8 dsp sun-dried tomato paste (see p. 101)
150ml (5fl oz) dry white wine or water (optional)

Put the lamb, fried onion, tomatoes, chillis, chilli sauce, half the beaten egg and the basil into a large bowl and mix well. Shape the mixture into 16 meatballs and coat with the remainder of the egg and the breadcrumbs. Fry in 2 dsp hot oil for 10 minutes turning occasionally.

While the lamb is cooking, prepare the sauce. Heat oil in a saucepan, add the onion, garlic and tomato paste. Thin sauce, if desired, by adding the wine or water. Heat thoroughly and keep warm while the spaghetti is cooked.

Cook the spaghetti in oiled and salted water for 10 minutes, then drain and arrange on a warm serving dish. Place the meatballs in the centre of the dish and pour over the hot sauce.

Pasta with Scallops

A delightful, unusual starter that combines pasta, scallops and a citrus-flavoured butter. Vary the butter flavour if you wish, by using lemon or orange in place of lime. This dish can be made in advance, stored in the fridge for 24 hours and then reheated under a grill.

[*Serves 3*]

60g (2oz) butter or margarine
juice of 1 lime
1 tsp lime rind, grated
6 large (king) scallops
1 bulb Florence fennel, shredded
2 dsp cream
4 dsp dry vermouth
1l (2 pt) water
½ tsp salt
1 dsp oil
125g (4oz) angel hair pasta
60g (2oz) wholemeal breadcrumbs
2oz mozarella or Gruyere cheese (optional)
sprigs dill, slices of lime and chopped spring onions to garnish

Mix together the butter, lime juice and rind. Set aside.

To prepare the scallops: open the shells, ideally with an oyster knife, and discard the top shell, remove the white muscle and red coral. Discard the membrane and dark organs, cut the small crescent-shaped muscle from the white meat and discard. Wash the meat, coral and shell thoroughly and pat dry. Brush the grill with a little of the lime butter, then grill the scallops and corals for 2 minutes on each side.

Heat two-thirds of the lime butter in a small pan, add the fennel and cook gently but do not allow to brown. Season to taste, reduce heat, add the cream and vermouth and mix well.

Boil the water in a large pot, add the salt, oil and then the pasta. Cook for 4 minutes. Drain and arrange on the scallop shells. Place the scallops on top of the pasta and the pour the sauce over.

Mix the breadcrumbs with the remaining lime butter and spinkle this and the cheese over the scallops before browning under a grill. Garnish and serve hot.

7

Game for Christmas

G ame in its many splendid forms is now available from plentiful sources. I feel that it is time to give the turkey a break and fill the festive tables with wonderful game dishes using venison, pheasant, duck and goose.

Recipes

· *A Christmas Goose* · *Glazed Roast Duck with an Orange and Nut Stuffing*
· *Rich Pheasant and Mushroom Casserole* · *Exotic Turkey Surprise*
· *A Game Terrine* · *Roast Haunch of Venison* · *Christmas Croustade*
· *Spiced Red Cabbage* · *Sage, Onion and Apple Stuffing*
· *Charred Vegetables with Olive Oil and Garlic*
· *Red Onion and Cranberry Marmalade* · *Marbled Apple and Redcurrant Sauce*
· *Cranberry Salsa* · *Gratin of Christmas Fruits*
· *Shimmering Clementine Jelly with a Medley of Christmas Fruits*

A Christmas
Goose

Goose, rich and slightly gamey in flavour, was once the traditional Christmas roast. However, because it is often much more expensive than turkey and provides less meat (the chances of having some left over for boxing day are slight) its popularity has dwindled. Fresh goose should have firm meat, a plump breast and be springy to the touch. Allow 1lb per person and avoid the larger, heavier birds as they are often too fatty for roasting. I prefer to cook the stuffing separately, as I find that the goose fat tends to dominate all other ingredients with its strong flavour. It is, however, an ideal fat in which to roast potatoes.

[Serves 8]

5kg (10lb) goose
2 apples, halved
2 onions, halved
300ml (10fl oz) cider
4 leaves fresh sage (or 1 tsp dried)
1 tsp cinnamon
1 tsp salt
2 dsp redcurrant jelly, softened

Wipe the bird, inside and out, with kitchen paper and remove any lumps of goose fat from around the cavity. Soak the apples and onions in a bowl with the cider, sage and cinnamon for at least 30 minutes. Then pack the fruit and herbs into the cavity of the goose.

Preheat oven to gas mark 7, 425°F, 220°C. Wipe the bird again to make sure the skin is perfectly dry: this is important if the goose is to become crispy. Prick the skin on the breast and legs with a skewer so that the fat can drain off during cooking. Be careful not to prick the flesh too deeply or you will lose the well-flavoured meat juices . Rub salt all over the goose and place, breast side up, on a trivet in a large roasting tin, then put into the oven for 30 minutes. Turn the goose over, reduce the temperature to gas mark 4, 350°F, 180°C and cook for 1 hour, basting occasionally. Then turn the goose again, dust with a little flour and brush with the redcurrant jelly. Raise the temperature to gas mark 6, 400°F, 200°C and roast for another 20 minutes. Transfer to a heated platter.

Serve with sage, onion and apple stuffing (see p. 120), charred vegetables in olive oil and garlic (p. 121) and marbled apple and redcurrant sauce (p. 124).

Previous page: Glazed Roast Duck

Glazed Roast Duck with an Orange and Nut Stuffing

Duck is a tasty option for Christmas dinner whether you are cooking a mild-flavoured, farmyard duck or a dark-fleshed, wild mallard. A duck for roasting should not be too bony or fatty: remember that 2kg (4lb) duck will only serve 4 people.

There are endless ways to roast a duck but I prefer the more traditional method of roasting with a tangy stuffing which creates moisture inside the bird while cooking.

[Serves 4]

150ml (5fl oz) boiling water
125g (4oz) couscous
juice and rind 1 orange
1 stalk celery, finely chopped
½ red onion, finely chopped
60g (2oz) pecan nuts or walnuts, toasted
½ tsp cinnamon
1 tsp coriander seeds, crushed
pinch salt and pepper
2kg (4lb) duck
2 Seville oranges, halved
2 dsp brandy (optional)
1 tsp salt

ORANGE GLAZE
150ml (5fl oz) water
125 (4oz) granulated sugar
juice and rind 4 clementines

Prepare the stuffing by pouring the boiling water over the couscous. Leave it for five minutes until it swells and softens slightly. Add the orange juice and rind, celery, onion, nuts, cinnamon, coriander seeds and seasoning and mix well.

Preheat oven to gas mark 5, 375°F, 180°C. Stuff the couscous mixture into the neck cavity of the duck and place the oranges halves (soaked in brandy, if liked) inside the main cavity. Rub the skin of the duck with the salt, prick the surface with a fork and place on a roasting rack.

Make the orange glaze by boiling the water, sugar, juice and rind of the clementines until it forms a thick syrup. Brush over the duck. Roast the duck for 1 hour (10 minutes per lb plus 15 minutes).

Rich Pheasant and Mushroom Casserole

This is an ideal way to cook rich, gamey pheasant, and, combined with other festive ingredients, this dish is especially good to serve when entertaining. To make a game stock simply follow the recipe for chicken stock (see p. 21) substituting game carcasses or bones for the chicken.

[Serves 4]

1 tbsp vegetable oil
30g (1oz) butter
2 oven-ready pheasants, jointed
30g (1oz) flour
250g (8oz) small onions, whole
250g (8oz) small mushrooms, whole
250g (8oz) chestnuts, shelled and peeled
1 dsp redcurrant jelly
150ml (5fl oz) full-bodied red wine
2 dsp port
rind of 1 orange, roughly chopped
800ml (1½pt) game stock
30g (1oz) plain flour blended with 2 dsp warm water (optional)
1 tsp redcurrant jelly (optional)

Heat the oil and butter in a large saucepan, toss the pheasant joints in the flour then brown on all sides. Remove from the saucepan. Put the onions, mushrooms and chestnuts into the saucepan and fry gently for several minutes. Add the redcurrant jelly, wine, port, orange rind and stock and stir well. Return the pheasant joints to the saucepan and either cook the casserole on the hob or in the oven for 1½ hours. I prefer this dish when cooked in the oven (gas mark 5, 375°F, 190°C).

If you like you can thicken the gravy a little by adding the flour and water mixture or enrich the colour by adding 1 extra tsp of redcurrant jelly just before serving. Serve garnished with fresh parsley, thyme or rosemary accompanied with spiced red cabbage (see p. 119).

Exotic Turkey Surprise

Despite the emphasis on game in this chapter, I have decided to include this very popular recipe as it is a very tasty way to use left-over turkey. The combination of white breast meat and brown leg meat works well in this dish.

[Serves 6-8]

2 dsp olive oil
1 onion, finely chopped
2 clove garlic, sliced
375g (12oz) long grain rice
1l (2 pt) vegetable or chicken stock
500g (1lb) turkey pieces, cooked
5 strands saffron soaked in 2 dsp boiling water
1 dsp spring onions, finely chopped
1 green pepper, finely chopped
2 dsp caramelised orange peel (see p. 77)
150ml (5fl oz) dry white wine
salt and pepper
60g (2oz) pistachio nuts, roughly chopped
2 dsp parsley

Heat the olive oil in a large saucepan and fry the onion and garlic until softened. Add the rice, stir until well-coated, then add the stock and simmer until the rice is almost cooked. Add the turkey pieces, saffron, spring onions, green pepper, caramelised orange peel, wine and seasoning and stir gently. Reduce the heat and cook for 7 minutes.

Serve hot garnished with pistachio nuts and finely chopped parsley. This dish is particularly good served with a green salad and crusty bread.

A Game
Terrine

A classic pate or terrine combines meat, spices, liver and plenty of seasoning. Whether it is coarse or smooth depends on how finely the ingredients are chopped or how long they are processed in a blender, and is a matter of preference. The flavour of pigeon breast give this dish a light gamey flavour.

Make the terrine 2-3 days in advance to allow the flavours plenty of time to combine. This is good for a festive buffet table or sliced and served as a starter.

[Serves 6-8]

250g (8oz) chicken livers, washed and trimmed
300g (10oz) belly of pork, rind removed and roughly chopped
1 dsp green peppercorns
4 juniper berries, crushed
4 pigeon breasts, roughly chopped
2 dsp sherry or brandy
rind 1 orange
1 clove garlic
2 shallots or small onions, finely chopped
1 egg, lightly beaten
salt and pepper
1 tsp fresh parsley, thyme or rosemary
2 dsp fresh cranberries (optional)
10 slices streaky bacon

Put the chicken livers and pork into a food processor and pulse until coarsely blended. Add the peppercorns and juniper berries and mix well. Put the pigeon pieces into a bowl with the sherry, orange rind, garlic and shallots. Leave to marinade for 1 hour then add to the pork and chicken livers along with the egg, seasoning, herbs and cranberries.

Preheat oven to gas mark 3, 325°F, 160°C. Grease a 1lb paté tin well and line with the slices of bacon, making sure that they spill out over the sides. Spoon the pate mixture in, press down well and fold in the overlapping strips of bacon. Cover with aluminium foil and place the tin in a roasting dish. Add enough boiling water to come half-way up the side of the pate tin and cook for 1½ hours. When cooked the pate will have shrunk from the sides of the tin and the juices will run clear. Cool and store in the fridge until required.

Overleaf: Game Terrine (left) and Haunch of Venison (right)

Roast Haunch of Venison

Venison is very lean and unless it is well-marinated, very gently cooked and basted frequently, it will dry out during roasting. This cut is probably best value for roasting, and comes from the top of the leg.

[Serves 6-8]

MARINADE
1 onion, chopped
1 carrot, chopped
1 stalk of celery, chopped
bunch thyme
1 dsp green peppercorns
300ml (10fl oz) red wine
1kg (2lb) haunch of venison, boned and rolled
2 dsp butter

SAUCE
300ml (10fl oz) meat juices
15g (½oz) plain flour
15g (½oz) butter
1 tsp thyme, rosemary or parsley, finely chopped

To prepare the venison: mix the onion, carrot, celery, thyme, peppercorns and red wine together. Place the venison in a large bowl and pour the marinade over. Cover and set aside for at least 6 hours, turning occasionally.

Preheat oven to gas mark 6, 400°F, 200°C. Heat the oil in a roasting dish, add the venison and brown before adding the marinade. Cover the roasting dish and roast for 1 hour.

To make the sauce: strain the meat juices from the roasting dish add the flour, butter and herbs and mix well.

Transfer the venison to a warmed serving platter and carve. Serve hot with the sauce. This dish goes particularly well with simple vegetables; try steamed baby potatoes and braised fennel or celery.

Christmas Croustade

A vegetarian alternative for the Christmas dinner. I like the combination of ribbons of vegetables and the garlic flavoured crust.

[Serves 8]

CROUSTADE
60g (2oz) butter
1 dsp olive oil
1 dsp spring onion, very finely chopped
2 cloves garlic, chopped
125g (4oz) chestnuts, cooked and chopped
300g (10oz) white breadcrumbs
1 egg, lightly beaten

FILLING
60g (2oz) butter
500g (1lb) mushrooms, sliced
2 spring onions, chopped
2 cloves garlic
1 large parsnip, blanched and finely sliced
1 courgette, finely sliced
100ml (3fl oz) red wine
1 dsp arrowroot blended with 2 dsp water
2 tsp fresh thyme
1 dsp parsley, finely chopped

To make the croustade: melt the butter in a large saucepan with the oil. Add the spring onions and garlic and fry for 2 minutes before adding the chestnuts. Continue cooking, then add the breadcrumbs and lightly beaten egg and mix well. Transfer two-thirds of the mixture into a loose-bottomed, 22cm (9 inch) cake tin, press well into the base and up the sides, then leave to cool.

Preheat oven to gas mark 5, 375°F, 190°C. Prepare the filling: melt the butter in a saucepan and add the mushrooms, spring onions and garlic. Cook for 4 minutes then reserve 3 dsp of the liquid. Add the parsnips, courgette, red wine, arrowroot and chopped thyme to the saucepan, mix well and cook gently for 6 minutes. Allow to cool slightly before transferring the mixture to the croustade case. Spoon over the reserved liquid, then sprinkle with parsley before covering with the remaining croustade mixture. Bake in the oven for 40 minutes.

Spiced Red Cabbage

Red cabbage requires a much longer cooking time than green cabbage. I find that a good red wine vinegar gives this dish a richer and more pleasant flavour than an ordinary malt vinegar.

[Serves 6]

1 dsp cooking oil
2cm- (1 inch-) cube of root ginger, finely chopped
1 small onion, finely sliced
2 stalks celery, finely chopped
½ medium-sized red cabbage, shredded
175g (6oz) cooking apples, peeled and sliced
125g (4oz) demerara sugar
750ml (1½pt) water or vegetable stock
salt and pepper
4 dsp red wine or red wine vinegar

Heat the oil in a large saucepan with the ginger, then add the onion and saut for 3 minutes. Add the celery and cook for 1 minute. Add the shredded cabbage, apples and sugar, mixing well before adding the stock and seasoning. Simmer on a low heat for 1 hour. Add the red wine just before serving, heat through and serve piping hot.

Spiced Red Cabbage

Sage, Onion and Apple Stuffing

Sage and onion is the traditional stuffing for turkey, but I have combined it with apples to make an ideal stuffing for roast goose. Because goose is so rich, I prefer a stuffing with plenty of flavour rather than the potato stuffing which is so often served with roast goose.

[Serves 8]

30g (1oz) butter, melted
1 large onion, finely chopped
juice and rind of 1 lemon
1 large cooking apple, peeled and chopped
250g (8oz) white breadcrumbs
125 (4oz) sausagemeat
1 goose liver, finely chopped (optional)
2 tsp fresh sage, chopped (or 1tsp dried)
1 egg

Preheat oven to gas mark 6, 400°F, 200°C. Melt the butter in a pan and fry the onion until soft. Put the lemon juice into a bowl and toss the apple pieces to help retain their colour. Add the onions and all the other ingredients and mix well. Transfer to an ovenproof dish and cook in the oven for 30 minutes.

Serve hot.

Charred Vegetables with Olive Oil and Garlic

This is my favourite way of cooking vegetables. Not only do they retain their colour, flavour and nutrients, but they also develop a lovely crispy texture. Best of all they are easy to prepare!

[Serves 8]

4 dsp olive oil
500g (1lb) small potatoes, washed and roughly chopped
4 parsnips (or 2 parsnips and 2 carrots), peeled and roughly chopped
250g (8oz) spring onion bulbs
4 cloves of garlic
salt and pepper
1 tsp paprika
2 tbsp red wine vinegar

Preheat oven to gas mark 6, 400°F, 200°C. Heat the oil in a roasting tin. Simmer the potatoes and parsnips in water for 5 minutes, then add to the hot oil along with the spring onions, garlic, salt and pepper. Ensure the vegetables are well-coated with the oil then roast in the oven for 1 hour until golden and crispy. Sprinkle with paprika and red wine vinegar and return to the oven for 5 minutes.
    Serve hot.

Red Onion and Cranberry Marmalade

This tasty marmalade is extremely versatile: it can be used as a relish and eaten hot or cold, the sharp zesty flavour is the perfect accompaniment to game meats. Replace the red onions and red wine with Spanish onions and white wine, if you prefer.

[Serves 6-8]

2 dsp oil
4 red onions, finely chopped
salt and pepper
125g (4oz) soft brown sugar
300ml (10fl oz) red wine
1 dsp wine vinegar
1 tsp crushed coriander seeds
125g (4oz) cranberries

Heat the oil in a saucepan and fry the onions for 8 minutes, being careful not to burn them. Add the seasoning, sugar, wine, vinegar and coriander seeds, and simmer for 15 minutes. Add the cranberries and simmer for a further 10 minutes or until they have softened and popped. Reduce the mixture until it resembles marmalade then remove from the heat. When cool, pour into sterilised, airtight jars and store in the fridge.

Marbled Apple and Redcurrant Sauce

Apple or redcurrant sauces are traditional accompaniments to game. This marbled sauce not only looks wonderful, it also tastes terrific.

[Serves 8]

juice 1 lemon
60g (2oz) soft brown sugar
150ml (5fl oz) water
4 dsp dry white wine (optional)
4 cooking apples, peeled, cored and cut into wedges
4 dsp redcurrant jelly, mixed with 2 dsp water
½ tsp cinnamon

Heat the lemon juice, sugar, water and wine until boiling, then add the apples. Reduce the heat, cover and leave to simmer very slowly until frothing. Pour the apple sauce into a sauceboat.

In a separate saucepan, heat the diluted redcurrant jelly and cinnamon until boiling. Remove from the heat and pour on top of the apple sauce. Swirl with a fork to give a marbled appearance.

Cranberry Salsa

The colour and flavour of this salsa combines well with the texture of cold meats at Christmas time, be they turkey duck or ham. A sharp, sweet relish of this type can be made in advance and stored in an airtight jar for up to 1 week.

[Serves 6]

1 dsp granulated sugar
150ml (5fl oz) water
250g (8oz) cranberries
1 tsp chilli sauce
1 small red onion, finely chopped
2 red plums, stones removed and cubed
1 dsp parsley, finely chopped

Bring the sugar and water to the boil then add the cranberries, chilli sauce, onion and plums. Simmer for 10 minutes over a low heat ensuring the fruit does not lose its shape or colour.

Serve hot or cold sprinkled with parsley.

Gratin of Christmas Fruits

The fruit for this pudding can be varied—use whatever is in season combined with a few berries (fresh or frozen).

[Serves 12]

6 clementines, peeled and sliced
2 pears, peeled and sliced
4 kiwi fruit, peeled and sliced
250g (8oz) grapes (black and green)
125g (4oz) redcurrants
125g (4oz) caster sugar
3 egg yolks
1 dsp cornflour mixed with 2 dsp water
few drops vanilla essence
2 dsp white wine
2 dsp Cointreau or orange juice
1 dsp whipped cream
1 dsp demerara sugar
2 tbsp toasted almonds, flaked
60g (2oz) icing sugar
1 tsp cinnamon powder

Place the fruit in an ovenproof dish and dust with one-quarter of the caster sugar. (If you like, you can poach the fruit first for 5 minutes over a low heat.) Whisk the egg yolks and remaining caster sugar in a bowl over a pan of warm, but not boiling, water until creamy and fluffy. Add the cornflour, vanilla and white wine and beat for 10 minutes over warm water until the sauce loses its eggy flavour. Remove from the heat and allow to cool before adding the liqueur or orange juice. Beat in the cream then pour over the fruits and dust with demerara sugar and almonds. Mix the icing sugar and cinnamon together then sprinkle on top and heat gently under a grill for 2 minutes until the sugar topping has caramelised. Serve hot.

Shimmering Clementine Jelly with a Medley of Christmas Fruits

This clear shimmering jelly, flavoured with seasonal clementine oranges and served with a medley of Christmas fruits is a refreshing finale to any Christmas meal.

[Serves 6-8]

CLEMENTINE JELLY
juice and rind 1 lemon
300ml (10fl oz) orange juice
rind 2 clementines
250g (8oz) caster sugar
750ml (1½pt) water
1 egg white, beaten (optional)
egg shells, washed and crushed (optional)
3 sachets gelatine dissolved in 4 dsp water

MEDLEY OF FRUITS
125g (4oz) caster sugar
300ml (10fl oz) water
pinch nutmeg
juice of ½ lemon
2 peaches, peeled and cut into segments
1 small melon, cut into chunks
125g (4oz) each, green and black grapes, de-seeded and halved
2 oranges, peeled and cut into segments
150ml (5fl oz) champagne or sparkling wine (optional)

Put the lemon juice and rind, orange juice and clementine rind, sugar and water into a saucepan and bring to a boil. Be careful not to overboil as the concentrated flavour of the oranges will be spoiled. Remove from the heat and strain through muslin into a bowl to remove the peel. A handy tip for a crystal clear jelly is the addition of a beaten egg white and crushed, washed egg shells to the mixture before it is strained. Add the gelatine and mix well. Pour into a mould and leave overnight in a cool place to set. When set remove from the mould by dipping in very hot water for a few seconds and inverting onto a plate.

To prepare the medley of fruits: heat the sugar, water, nutmeg and lemon juice in a small saucepan until bubbling. Leave to cool, then add the fruits and champagne or sparkling wine and mix well.

Serve on a platter with the jelly surrounded by the fruits.